W9-AUA-949

FAMOUS NATIVE AMERICANS™

Chief Ouray
Ute Peacemaker

Diane Shaughnessy
Jack Carpenter

The Rosen Publishing Group's

PowerKids Press™
New York

Published in 1997 by The Rosen Publishing Group, Inc.
29 East 21st Street, New York, NY 10010

Copyright © 1997 by The Rosen Publishing Group, Inc.

All rights reserved. No part of this book may be reproduced in any form without permission in writing from the publisher, except by a reviewer.

First Edition

Book Design: Danielle Primiceri

Photo Credits: Cover, pp. 4, 11, 15 © UPI/Corbis-Bettmann; pp. 7, 8, 16 (right) © Archive Photos; p. 8 (left) © Corbis-Bettmann; p. 12 © Corbis-Bettmann; p. 14 © FPG International; p. 19 © Frank Leslie's Illustrated Newspaper/Corbis; p. 20 © Sally Morgan; Ecoscene/Corbis.

Shaughnessy, Diane.
    Chief Ouray : Ute peacemaker / Diane Shaughnessy, Jack Carpenter.
        p.   cm. — (Famous Native Americans)
    Includes index.
    Summary: A biography of the Ute Indians' great peacemaker whose tribe retained their land and freedom until his death in 1880.
    ISBN 0-8239-5108-1
    1. Ouray—Juvenile literature. 2. Ute Indians—Kings and Rulers—Biography—Juvenile literature. 3. Ute Indians—History—Juvenile literature. [1. Ouray. 2. Ute Indians—Biography. 3. Indians of North America—Biography.] I. Title. II. Series.
E99.U80975 1997
978.8'0049745'0092—dc21   97-221
                                                                             CIP
                                                                             AC

Manufactured in the United States of America

Contents

Ouray of the Utes

Ouray (OO-ray) was born in 1833. He grew up to become a great peacemaker for the **Ute** (YOOT) Indians. When he was fourteen years old, Ouray learned about the troubles of the **Pueblo** (PWEH-bloh) Indians in New Mexico. They

◀ *Ouray would one day keep the promise that he made to himself and his people.*

The Utes lived in what are now the states of Utah, Wyoming, and Colorado.

refused (ree-FYOOZD) to give up their land and freedom and live the way the U.S. **government** (GUH-vern-ment) wanted them to. So the government sent soldiers to hurt them. Ouray didn't want that to happen to the Utes. He made a promise to himself and to his people that he would do everything he could to keep the Utes safe and free.

Living in the Desert

The Ute American Indian tribe once lived in the Great Basin area of the Rocky Mountains. The Great Basin runs through the states of Colorado, Utah, and Wyoming. Some of the land was good for growing food, but most of it was dry desert. In order for the Utes to **survive** (ser-VYV), they learned to live off the land. They gathered and ate roots, seeds, and insects. Sometimes they hunted animals, such as antelope, jackrabbits, squirrels, and other small animals.

The Utes were skilled at finding and hunting for food in their dry desert land. ▶

Living in Peace

The Utes lived in peace on their land for many years. When Ouray was a boy, many white **settlers** (SET-tul-erz) began to travel West to find new land to live on and farm. But because the Utes' land was so dry, very few settlers wanted to live there. Ouray and the Utes felt lucky that they were safe from settlers.

For many years, the Utes were safe from white settlers because their homeland was so hard to live on.

9

Ouray Becomes a Man

When Ouray was a young man, he married a woman named Black Mare. They were happy together. But Black Mare died while giving birth to their son. Ouray asked a young woman named Chipeta to help him care for his son. Ouray and Chipeta soon fell in love and were married. Chipeta was 16, and Ouray was 26. They stayed together until Ouray died, 21 years later.

In most Native American tribes, it was part of the woman's job to take care of the children. ▶

Newcomers

The Utes first met white people during the 1500s. **Explorers** (ex-PLOR-erz) from Spain decided that they wanted the Utes' land. The Utes refused to give up their land. They drove the explorers away. Three hundred years later, the U.S. government learned that there was copper on the Utes' land. The government wanted the land for settlers, who would **mine** (MYN) the copper. Soldiers soon arrived. After many battles, the Utes were forced to give up their land and move onto **reservations** (reh-zer-VAY-shunz).

Many settlers traveled West in search of metals, such as copper and gold. These men are "panning," or looking, for gold.

Ute Spokesman

The U.S. government was happy to have the Utes' land. But they were afraid that the Utes would attack the white settlers who had moved there. They learned that a young Ute man, Ouray, knew how to speak several languages, including English. Ever since he had made his promise, Ouray had learned all about

14

the U.S. government laws and how they **affected** (uh-FEK-ted) the Native Americans in North America. The government wanted Ouray to help them keep peace between the Utes and the white settlers.

Chief Ouray helped make sure that the settlers didn't take more Ute land than was agreed upon. ▶

Peacemaker

The government made Ouray a chief and asked him to talk to the Utes. The Utes were angry because they had not chosen Ouray as chief or as their **spokesperson** (SPOHKS-per-sun). But Ouray was calm and **honest** (ON-est). He was able to get the Utes and the government to sign peace **treaties** (TREE-teez). The Utes were allowed to keep their land and freedom. And the white settlers were allowed to mine for copper. This peace lasted for many years. Chief Ouray was happy that he had kept his promise to himself and his people.

The Utes did not choose Ouray as their chief. But as chief, Ouray made sure that the Utes could keep their land.

Broken Treaties

Chief Ouray died in 1880, at the age of 47. Around this time, the government decided to **claim** (CLAYM) the rest of the Ute land for white settlers. Once again, the government sent soldiers to force the Utes onto smaller reservations. But now Chief Ouray wasn't there to help keep the peace. The Utes had no one to turn to. The peace treaties that Chief Ouray had kept strong for so many years were broken.

Without Chief Ouray to help keep the peace treaties, the Utes were forced to move onto reservations. ▶

Utah and Colorado

The Utes were moved to reservations in what are now Utah and Colorado. Utah, whose name comes from the Ute tribe, means "high up" or "land of the sun." Today, the Utes live on three reservations in Utah and Colorado. Their way of life has changed. Today, they farm and raise cattle rather than hunt and gather their food.

The name "Utah" comes from the Ute tribe. Utah is one of the states in which the Utes live on reservations today. This is a photo of Bryce Canyon, an area of Utah that is very difficult to live in or travel through.

Keeping Traditions

Although they faced many of the same challenges as the Pueblo Indians, the Utes did not suffer the same **fate** (FAYT) as long as Chief Ouray was alive.

Chief Ouray helped make sure that the Utes and their **traditions** (truh-DISH-unz) would survive. Many Utes still do the same dances, follow the same customs, and pray the same prayers as the Utes did during Chief Ouray's time.

Chief Ouray was able to keep his promise to himself and his people.

Glossary

affect (uh-FEKT) To have an impact on something or someone.

claim (CLAYM) To demand as your own.

explorer (ex-PLOR-er) A person who travels over little-known lands.

fate (FAYT) What happens to a person or a group of people.

government (GUH-vern-ment) The person or people who run a country.

honest (ON-est) Truthful.

mine (MYN) To dig into the earth in order to take out metals.

Ouray (OO-ray) The name of a Ute chief.

Pueblo (PWEH-bloh) One group of Native Americans.

refuse (ree-FYOOZ) To say no to.

reservation (reh-zer-VAY-shun) An area of land set aside by the government for the Indians to live on.

settler (SET-tul-er) A person who sets up house in a new place.

spokesperson (SPOHKS-per-sun) A person who speaks for others.

survive (ser-VYV) To keep living.

tradition (truh-DISH-un) A way of doing something that is passed down from parent to child.

treaty (TREE-tee) An agreement between two groups of people.

Ute (YOOT) One group of Native Americans.

Big Valley Eleme...
202 - 18th Stree...
Rupert, ID 83350

Index